THE NEW CROSS MASSACRE STORY

THE NEW CROSS MASSACRE STORY

Interviews with John La Rose
prologue by Linton Kwesi Johnson
epilogue by Gus John

For Elizabeth
Peace + Progress,
Gus John

New Beacon Books

George Padmore Institute

This edition published 2011 by New Beacon Books Ltd.,
76 Stroud Green Road, London N4 3EN for the George Padmore Institute

The New Cross Massacre Story: interviews with John La Rose published 1984 by the Alliance of the Black Parents Movement, Black Youth Movement and the Race Today Collective.

This booklet is published as part of the ***Dream To Change The World Project***. This five year HLF funded project began at the George Padmore Institute in June 2010. Its purpose is to make available to the public the personal archives of John La Rose, the GPI's founding chairman.

ISBN 978 1 873201 31 2

Printed by Imprint Digital, Exeter, England

CONTENTS

13 OF OUR
CHILDREN
MURDERED
JAN '81
ANDREW GOODING
OWEN THOMPSON
PAUL RUDDOCK
YVONNE RUDDOCK
PATRICIA JOHNSON
13

WE HAVE NOT FORGOTTEN

PROLOGUE BY LINTON KWESI JOHNSON
MARCH 2011

' ... at the present time blacks are really very much inside British society ... no longer on the periphery'

– John La Rose, 2003

The most significant date in the history of the black experience in Britain during the second half of the twentieth century is the year 1981. It began inauspiciously in the early hours of 18 January with a racist arson attack on a sixteenth birthday part in south-east London, which resulted in the deaths of thirteen young black people and twenty-six revellers suffering serious injuries. The response of the police, aided and abetted by sections of the media, with the implicit approval of the government, was to use their power to deny justice to the survivors of the fire, the bereaved and the dead. The shock, sorrow and outrage felt by black people throughout the country found expression in concrete political action. On 2nd March, some six weeks after the fire, the New Cross Massacre Action Committee, chaired by the late John La Rose, mobilised 20,000 people for a march through the streets of London. That Black People's Day of Action was an unprecedented demonstration of black political power. It was a wake up call for the authorities, a watershed moment that signalled a paradigm shift in race relations in the UK. Moreover, with the Day of Action came a leap in Black British consciousness of the power to bring about change.

Opposite: *Flowers placed outside 439 New Cross Road, scene of the New Cross Massacre Fire.*

Then in April came the uprisings which began with the Brixton riots and spread to inner cities throughout the country. After three decades of racial oppression and marginalisation, second and third generation young blacks made it abundantly clear that things would have to change. We would not longer tolerate being treated as third class citizens – if citizens at all; we were no longer prepared to remain on the periphery of British society, and were willing to fight fire with fire.

In 1981 Britain was undergoing deep structural changes in the wake of the economic crises of the 1970s. It was a turbulent time of class conflict. Racism was rampant and racial prejudice permeated every institution of the state. The new Conservative government of the day, led by Margaret Thatcher, had launched an assault on the gains won by the British working classes after the Second World War. It was a time of racial tension, exacerbated by right-wing politicians like Thatcher, whose anti-immigrant rhetoric fanned the flames of hatred and emboldened racist and fascist organisations. By then there was a mass movement of politicised young blacks and several autonomous organisations engaged in the struggle for racial equality and social justice.

Racist acts of terror against blacks and Asians did not begin with the New Cross arson attack, but coincided with Caribbean migration to the UK in the 1950s. There were the Notting Hill and Nottingham riots of 1958 and 1959, where blacks fought back, and the murder, also in Notting Hill, of Antiguan worker Kelso Cochrane. After the Conservative Member of Parliament, Enoch Powell, made his infamous inflammatory 'rivers of blood' speech in 1968, demanding the repatriation of black Commonwealth immigrants, there was a marked increase in racist attacks and the rise of fascist organisations such as the National Front, the British Movement and Column 88. In 1971, a decade before the New Cross fire, there was a similar arson attack on a West Indian party in Forest Hill in south-east London where, luckily, no one died. The New Cross area, in particular the London borough of Lewisham, was notorious as a hotbed of National Front activism and racist arson attacks. In 1977, the Moonshot, a black youth and community centre, was fire-bombed. That year Lewisham also witnessed street battles between National Front supporters on the one hand and anti-racists from the Anti-Nazi League, supported by black youths, on the other. In 1978, the Albany Theatre in Deptford was fire-bombed in a suspected racist attack, as was the Lewisham Way Centre in 1980. The New Cross fire was, therefore, not an isolated act of barbarism, but the latest and most devastating in a history of racist terror.

There were two inquests into the New Cross fire, both of which returned open verdicts. If the first, held with indecent haste just three months after the fire, was a travesty of justice where crucial evidence was suppressed by the coroner, then the second inquest, held in 2004, was a farce, as no new evidence was produced. However, on both occasions the police failed to convince the jury that the fire was the result of 'black on black' violence. The open verdicts have not allowed closure for the bereaved and the survivors of the fire, but the Black People's Day of Action and the uprisings that followed in 1981 and again in 1985 were harbingers of change. These dramatic demonstrations of black self empowerment left the Conservative government of the day with no alternative but to implement policies that would accelerate the emergence of a black middle class and a move towards inclusion.

The New Cross Massacre Story: Interviews with John La Rose is the only authoritative account of an important juncture in recent British history. As Chairman of the New Cross Massacre Action Committee (NCMAC), John La Rose was able to give a detailed account of the black communities' response to the fire, the formation of the NCMAC, the conduct of the police and their collaborators and the Black People's Day of Action. This publication also includes an appendix, with the 'Declaration of New Cross', the public statement made on the Black People's Day of Action; letters to the Prime Minister, the Commissioner of Police and the Speaker of the House of Commons; the Early Day Motion signed by some Labour Members of Parliament; a statement to the Press Association; the names of the thirteen young black people who died in the fire; and a public statement on the inquest and the appeal against the open verdict.

Documents and papers from the New Cross Massacre Action Committee's campaign for justice for the victims of the fire are stored in the archives of the George Padmore Institute and can be accessed by the public.

THE NEW CROSS MASSACRE STORY

Interviews with John La Rose

ANDREW GOODING
PATRICIA JOHNSON
16.5.1965 – 18.1.1981

INTRODUCTION

The largest and most effective demonstration of black political power in Britain over the last 30 years took place on Monday, March 2nd 1981. On that day 15-20,000 blacks, under the banner of the New Cross Massacre Action Committee, demonstrated through the streets of London. They were mobilised to protest the mishandling by police officers of investigations into the fire which claimed the lives of 13 young blacks at a birthday party held on January 17th/18th 1981 at the home of a West Indian family at 439, New Cross Road, South London. The demonstrators were also protesting the lies, distortions and misreporting in the British press on issues arising out of the fire, as well as the failure of the Thatcher government to respond sensitively to the incident.

John La Rose, publisher, writer and political activist, chaired the New Cross Massacre Action Committee. During the period of agitation and political mobilisation, La Rose gave several interviews to the media. We have selected two of these for publication. The first was originally published by the Trotskyite weekly, *Socialist Challenge* on June 17th 1981, and details not only the development and dynamics of the particular struggle, but outlines the general political position of the Alliance of the Black Parents Movement, the Black Youth Movement and the Race Today Collective to which La Rose belongs.

The second interview was published by the Caribbean Marxist journal, *Archipelago*, June 1983 Nos 3 & 4. *Archipelago* is a theoretical journal, published in France, and concentrates mainly on the struggles of Caribbean peoples for liberation from colonialism and imperialism.

Opposite: *Black Peoples Day of Action March, 2 March 1981*

The interview, which focuses on the events at New Cross, is set within the context of the black presence in Europe, our links with our countries of origin and our struggles for change in this part of the world.

The major issue, which arose out of the New Cross Massacre, is still to be resolved. Who was responsible for setting fire to that house and how was the fire actually set? To this day these questions are still to be answered, and despite the vast outlay of police resources, we are still in the dark. It is much more than that though. The New Cross Massacre Action Committee had to exercise every ounce of alertness and vigilance to prevent the police from framing a group of young blacks who were at the party.

Their initial attempt took the following form. The police were aware of the tremendous response on the part of black people to a call for a demonstration on March 2nd 1981 – the Black Peoples Day of Action. In the week prior, they detained a group of young blacks who attended the party and forced some of them to sign statements attributing the fire to a fight between the youths in a ground-floor front room of the house. It was a cynical ploy aimed at blaming blacks for the horrible and ghastly crime which led to the deaths of 13 black children. Some of the accused were very close and life long friends of the dead.

The New Cross Massacre Action Committee not only stopped this but exposed the ploy to the whole country. The police have not given up; they have simply changed tack. Theirs is a relentless drive to leave the impression that blacks killed blacks. Presently, they are asking the public to disregard the pages of detailed evidence which supported the fight theory. It was evidence which they themselves manufactured. No longer the youths in the front room. They, as well as others in the hallway, and even those on their way up and down the stairs and in the back room disappeared at the wave of a conjuror's wand. Instead, they place a black friend of the birthday girl's mother in the front room. Apparently he was jealous of his lover's behaviour at the party and set fire to the house. Having done that, he emigrated to the USA and cannot be found. It is perhaps the most remarkable turn around in the history of criminal investigations. Pages and pages of evidential statements have been dismantled and we guess that pages and pages of new evidence by original witnesses have been reconstructed. It is a pack of lies and the New Cross Massacre Action Committee will prove it at an opportune moment.

Over the last three years the police have entertained the black community with a cat and mouse game. Just at the time of each anniversary of the deaths, they announce that they are about to apprehend the person who caused the fire. Recently there has been some consistency though; they have stuck like a worn out gramophone record in the jealous lover groove. At one point the New Cross Massacre Action Committee had organised an International Commission of Enquiry. As the day approached, out came the banner headlines in the press that the culprit would be apprehended shortly. That was two years ago. Not wishing to complicate or indeed interfere with the concluding stages of the police investigations, the Enquiry was postponed indefinitely.

The point has finally arrived when large numbers of blacks and whites are aware that the police are bent, maliciously so, on leaving the taste in the mouths of all that a black person caused the fire. In order to achieve this they have dragged the name of one of the parents through muck and mire; they have systematically spread the most vicious personal gossip about the private lives of young and old alike; they have twisted arms to elicit the most obscure and irrelevant information; they have sought to taint the Fund Raising Committee with corruption only to be thwarted by the publication of audited accounts.

It is malice of the worst and most degenerate kind.

The New Cross Massacre Story remains a valid and comprehensive account of a tremendous moment in the struggles of black people in Britain for freedom.

Alliance of the Black Parents Movement, the Black Youth Movement and the Race Today Collective.

April 1984

Darcus Howe speaking at the Meeting in Deptford Town Hall to commemorate the first anniversary of the New Cross Massacre Fire.
Photo: Julian Stapleton

INTERVIEW WITH SOCIALIST CHALLENGE

17 JUNE 1981

How did you get involved in the events around the fire?
I was in a routine meeting of the Black Parents Movement when we heard the news and decided to investigate. Three of us saw Mrs Ruddock (who lost her children Yvonne and Paul) that same evening, and Alex Pascall of Black Londoners did an interview for his radio programme. We were present in the room when the interview took place.

In spite of her agony and suffering she spoke to us because she had already heard radio reports that weren't true. She said that it had been a peaceful party. There had been no fights. It was the first party she had given in the house. She'd made a special concession to her daughter, Yvonne for her 16th birthday and she was glad she had because she had never been so happy before. She was very clear about what she thought had happened – that it was a firebomb. Two police officers at different times had told her this.

Already a number of West Indian organisations and papers had been in the area: such as *West Indian World* and the West Indian Standing Conference. We weren't the only ones.

The WISC had already called a public meeting the following Sunday. We intervened and suggested that there should be a preparatory meeting on 20 January. 300 people attended. This established the New Cross Massacre Action Committee and part of its work became known as the Black People's Assembly.

People came from as far away as the Midlands. It really gave the black community some idea of what had taken place not from the press but from people like Lesley Morris and Carl Wright who were at the party.

A nurse who had received the victims at the hospital spoke. That meeting showed the extent of the concern in the community for what had taken place.

Who was involved in NCMAC?

You can imagine the range of voices on that question. The decision was that the Committee would be open to Asians, Africans and West Indians – all black people for the purpose of directing the campaign.

The Assembly should be open to all those who supported the general aims of the campaign. The Assembly made recommendations and the Committee took the decisions about how to carry them through.

PACM-Headstart (Pan African Congress Movement) said that only Africans and West Indian blacks should be involved. From the first meeting this position was rejected. In spite of this some Asians and whites were threatened. Stewards took action against it but we could never get a commitment from PACM-Headstart to stop this harassment.

How did the campaign develop?

We knew it would go through certain phases. The press had played down the issue after two days. So we knew that the attitude of the press and the state would be dependent on the reaction of the black community.

The public meeting on Sunday 25 January was important. 2000 people turned up and some came from further north – not just from the Midlands, but Bradford, Huddersfield, Leeds and Manchester.

Sybil Phoenix, a local community worker, planned a demonstration in collaboration with the police to go from the rally to 439 New Cross Road. Once there she began to sing 'We shall overcome'.

But this wasn't a civil rights movement like in the 1960s. They would like it to be but it isn't. Anyway the reggae songs are much more vital.

When she moved away from the house on the route she had planned with the police only 50 people followed her.

The others said no and remained blocking the road outside the house for 3 or 4 hours. This destroyed the plans of the police to bring the black community behind the Community Relations Councils and Commission for Racial Equality, in this struggle and campaign.

We see these in this struggle and campaign as a colonial office for blacks in British society. Their purpose is to undermine the independent struggle of blacks.

How do you see the Black Peoples Day of Action?

This was an historic event. The decision to hold it came from the NCMAC on 27 January. The decision was to show the determination of the black population that they will not be killed, maimed or injured with impunity and that if the state would not protect its citizens then the black population and its allies in the country would.

Can you say what you think of the inquiry and the next stage of the campaign.

The inquest was obviously an important event for the police. The press, like the *Observer* and the *Sunday Times* sought to tell the black community that what was being said about the massacre being a racist attack wasn't true. The truth was something else. The truth was the police story.

We knew that a grandstand play would be made at the inquest where the police would attempt to elaborate their theories in a way which would be convincing to the population and to the blacks who had demonstrated on the Black Peoples Day of Action on 2 March.

This plan failed because I don't think the police and the coroner and those behind them really realised the extent to which the NCMAC was prepared. It had been prepared since the 20 January when both the NCMAC and the Fact-Finding Commission was established.

This Commission investigated what had happened and it also found out about the methods that the police were using to obtain their information and their line of investigation.

Eventually all that became public knowledge at the time of the inquiry.

The police had a political motive in trying to prove that this was not a racist attack. If they had admitted it was a firebomb then it wouldn't have been 15-20,000 marching on the streets but 100,000. It was this they sought to prevent. It would be a march to protest police failure to stem racist attacks like the recent one in Coventry.

It is a matter for serious consideration that the coroner, Dr Davies, a leading coroner in Britain, should have shown bias and incompetence to the extent that he did. The parents sought an injunction against him for his summing up, the reading of police evidence rather than notes which he had failed to take. It was admitted by Justice Comyn that the coroner had acted with gross irregularity. The bias had been shown.

The open verdict was unsatisfactory to the families. On the evidence that had been shown it was clear that the police had failed to look for the truth about what had happened.

The police weren't satisfied with the verdict either. They had concentrated their efforts on proving their story of the fire starting as a result of a fight at the party. The parents immediately called for a new inquest and as soon as they receive the transcripts or the summing up they will lodge an appeal.

The New Cross Massacre Action Committee will be organising an International Commission of Inquiry within the next few weeks, after consultation around the country.

ACCIDENT OR ARSON?

The families in mourning began to feel that no one cared for their distress

The evening after the fire, Sunday 18 January, saw the first of the meetings that led to the formation of MAC, led by John La Rose and Darcus Howe, the latter a radical socialist involved with the Race Today collective in Brixton, which calls itself 'the voice of the black community in Britain'. MAC were soon organising meetings from which white people were often excluded.

Relations between the black community and the establishment rapidly began to go very sour. The bereaved families felt that the newspapers were giving far less coverage to the case than they would have done if the youngsters killed had been white. There was no message of sympathy from the Queen, and a letter from the Prime Minister arrived only five weeks later and then seemed concerned mainly with defending the police investigation. The families in mourning began to feel that no one cared for their distress. They compared this apparent indifference to the outpourings of sympathy for a young policeman who had lost a hand in an explosion at nearby Catford Police Station a year before.

Early on in the inquiry, the press began to print controversial information, given to them by the police, which was not freely available to the families of the dead. People read about the evidence of forensic scientists that the fire had been started by paint thinners or a similar liquid being ignited. This was consistent with the theory of a firebomb thrown in from outside, but the press stories were also claiming that the fire began in the centre of the room, not near the window. Press reports also said that Commander Graham Stockwell, the CID head for that area of London, had stated three days after the fire that there was 'no evidence which suggested a racial motive', and that an innocent explanation had been found for the man seen making a throwing motion and driving off in a hurry. But no precise details about this were made public before the inquest – which was not held until three months later.

The police had quickly understood the effect the affair could have on race relations, and had taken pains to try to set up good communications with the bereaved families. But there is a long history of conflict between the police and black people in the area, and the selective information that reached the press aroused suspicion that the police were not taking seriously the theory of a racialist attack. Commander John Smith, then head of P district of the Metropolitan Police, began to find that he could not even address meetings of local black people without being shouted down and derided. The atmosphere surrounding the inquiry into the cause of the fire went from bad to worse.

By early March 1981 the resentment had reached such a pitch that MAC was able to organise a demonstration that attracted several thousand people to protest about racialist attacks on black people, what they saw as sparse and biased media coverage of the tragedy, the apparent slowness of the police investigation and indifference from whites. The demonstration, on the afternoon of 2 March, was led by musicians and a symbolic coffin, followed by life-sized photographs of the dead carried aloft on placards. When police made a hasty decision to change the agreed route of the march – apparently because they feared disorder – the more unruly elements cut loose, pouring down Fleet Street chanting 'Freedom! Justice!' as they went. The window of a jeweller's shop was smashed; shoppers were pushed and knocked over. There were a few robberies, ugly scuffles with the police, involving injuries on both sides, and between 25 and 30 arrests.

The popular press, reporting the rally, concentrated on the disorder and violence by the fringe elements, thus beginning another downward spiral in the vicious circle of resentment between black people and the white establishment. The day inevitably caused a deterioration in relations with the police as well. When the extreme right-wing National Front planned a march in Deptford as a response, the Home Secretary, William Whitelaw, banned it for the sake of

Below: on the first day of the inquest into the fire, held at County Hall, the New Cross Massacre Action Committee demonstrates against the direction that was being taken by the police in the presentation of their evidence. The placard carried by the small child is a reference to police claims that Owen Thompson was accused by Wayne Doonter of having suggested that they 'set the place alight' after they had found nothing worthwhile to steal. In the witness box, Doonter denied all these allegations, insisting that he had given his statements to the police under pressure after they had told him that other boys had already 'confessed' to fighting. Photographs of the dead, with their names and dates, featured strongly in demonstrations outside County Hall.

832

833

'The Deptford Fire', published in Unsolved, *vol.4, issue 42, 1984. Picture shows the picket outside County Hall where the first inquest was held in April 1981.*

All the youths said that they had been bullied and coerced into making those statements which they retracted. Are there any moves to charge the police with illegal activity?
Not that I know of. What would happen is that the police would investigate themselves and find themselves without blemish, with no case to answer.

How do you see the problem of racist violence and right wing groups?
For the black community the most serious and violent attacks come from the police. The actions of the National Front and other right wing groups complement that violence.

The state confers its authority and arbitrary powers on the police.

The Blair Peach inquiry showed how the Special Patrol Group was itself acting illegally with all sorts of violent instruments against all those who they regarded as offensive to the state.

How should black people fight the police and right wing groups?
There are two ways. One is the way you fight in Brixton. You organise, attack and disappear because to expose yourself at all after an event like the Brixton insurrection is to invite virtual annihilation. Or like in New Cross where you can have a huge political effect on society by the nature of your political organisation.

I believe the most advanced form of warfare is political warfare, not military. There are sections of the black population who say that you have to be as organised as the police. I don't disagree with that but I see it as important to win over politically those sections of the working class who, like the black working class and unemployed, suffer at the hands of the police, the judges, the courts.

We have to organise politically to fight police violence – in terms of organising day by day against cases of repression.

Black political action defines itself in relation to the work place and in terms of its naked relationship to the state.

Most of the black youth and unemployed when they move against their oppression immediately come up against the state. So they're on the streets or in an insurrection like Bristol or Brixton.

If you're in the workplace you have your union meetings, then you have to find a way of getting around your district secretary and finally you're up against management. There are all these layers between you and your ultimate oppressor – the state.

The minute the black youth and unemployed act they come up against the oppressive nature of the state and they are very clear – this is Babylon.

And they have to deal with the gatemen of Babylon – the police, the army, the judges, the courts. It gives them a different sense of their politics.

It's not the same with the Asian working class. They have a strong middle class.

The West Indian community hasn't got an economically strong middle class. There is no part of the West Indian community that can regulate its conduct. It doesn't exist.

The state would like to create an effective group to control the black working class and unemployed. But it can't and therefore the black unemployed create a serious problem when they revolt.

What do you think of the role of anti-racist groups which seem to be usually white?
Yes, black people don't normally participate in them. I wouldn't say that they don't have a function.

Because racist violence comes from whites, then the extent to which these groups can mobilise white workers and sections of the white middle classes against these people then they can be important in creating alliances between the struggles of the black and white working classes. But if you expect the black working class to be part of these groups you misunderstand the nature of our struggles.

If by forming a white anti-racist group you think you are defending the black working class which is incapable of defending itself this is starting from the wrong assumption.

In a recent television programme Miriam Karlin of the Anti-Nazi League was talking about 'poor blacks'. But blacks don't see ourselves this way. We see ourselves as facing all sorts of economic, racial and cultural oppression and are quite capable of fighting our own battles.

In some industries two thirds of the workforce is black. Do you see that they have more force in society than the unemployed?
Yes, an issue of *Race Today* said, 'We are the majority at Fords'. Certain forms of conduct have been observed at Fords Dagenham, as when they had that internal insurrection a couple of years ago and broke the place up.

Where they have power over production, as in textiles, various parts of engineering works, service industries, it does confer on the black working class a power to influence the situation politically that we need to have. For example who have overthrown British Governments or forced them to make U-turns in recent times? Miners.

Tony Benn said recently that black people should come into the Labour Party, organise separately if they want to and affiliate as a body.

The 'Tory' state rules whoever is in the government – be it Labour or Conservative. You couldn't live in a colony as I did and believe that the Labour Party was a radical or anti-imperialist party.

The Labour Party has always been seen as an alternative that will staunch the rebellion of the working class when it becomes restive.

What makes the situation different now is this: that the crisis in the Labour Party is part of the crisis in society.

In my opinion the party has to split and split again to make it a reliable instrument of activity for the working class.

One supports the general direction of the Labour Party towards a radical socialist party. The situation that Tony Benn is part of will lead to a greater radicalisation and democratisation in the Labour Party and the trade unions which have been a functional part of the Labour Party.

These developments are of great importance for the black working class and unemployed as they are for the white. Black people may take up Benn's appeal when it becomes more real than it is at the moment.

Whatever else is said the problems facing the British state today are the Irish national liberation war, the unemployed and the restless working class. It is the coalescing of all these struggles that will make for serious change in Britain.

INTERVIEW WITH ARCHIPELAGO

JUNE 1983

John La Rose, from Trinidad, Joint-Director of the International Book Fair of Radical, Black and Third World Books, and Book Fair Festival week held in London annually; the first was in April 1982. He is a poet and publisher at New Beacon Books who has lived in the UK since 1961 He is a former executive of the Federated Workers Trade Union in Trinidad and Tobago, now part of the National Union of Government and Federated Workers, and former General Secretary of the West Indian Independence Party.

In 1966, he founded the Caribbean Artists' Movement together with Edward Kamau Brathwaite, historian, poet and critic, and Andrew Salkey, the novelist and poet. He produced the first reading of Aime Cesaire's *Cahiers d'un Retour au Pays Natal* in London at one of the sessions of this group in 1967. He has worked in films, television and theatre, producing the *Mangrove 9* film in 1972 with Franco Rosso. He founded the George Padmore School and the Black Parents Movement and is one of the leaders of the Black Alliance – an alliance of the three movements, the Black Parents Movement, the Black Youth Movement and the Race Today Collective formed in 1978. He is also the chairman of the New Cross Massacre Action Committee.

Just over two years ago, in January 1981, 13 black teenagers were burnt to death by fire in the house where they were celebrating a birthday in New Cross

(London). Dissatisfaction with the Metropolitan Police's handling of the inquiry into this fire, believed to be a criminal act, the work of fascists, led the black community to set up the New Cross Massacre Action Committee – of which you are the Chairman. Two months after the fire in March 1981, between 15,000 and 25,000 people, mainly black, marched from New Cross to central London in protest and April saw the outbreak of violent confrontation in Brixton, between the police and the community. Tell us what happened why and will it happen again? How far are factors like unemployment responsible – poverty, education –, and how far is the attitude of the police, racial discrimination...?

First, the New Cross Massacre Action Committee was formed at a meeting which was intended to be an ordinary committee meeting at which 300 people turned up on the 20th January. There was total outrage that something like this could have happened and one of the aspects of the outrage was that the authorities, or the police, had responded in the way they had to what was for us a holocaust or a massacre. The intention at that stage was to hold a public meeting on the 25th, the following Sunday, and that we would call a demonstration on that day so as to show the extent of the outrage felt by the black community against those who had perpetrated the acts as well as against the authorities who had not taken any serious view of what had occurred. Neither the Prime Minister, the Parliament, nor the media.

What relation do you see between the New Cross massacre and what happened 2 or 3 months later in Brixton?

The New Cross massacre gave rise to one of the historic moments of the history of the black community in Britain. On the 27th January it was decided to hold a New Cross Massacre Black People's Day of Action on Monday March 2nd 1981, approximately two months after the massacre had occurred. The purpose of that was to disrupt the working day – make the entire country aware that the black community will not stand for the kind of outrage and holocaust which had occurred. On that day, the march began in New Cross and ended in Hyde Park, approximately 12 miles. It took about 7 hours for that march to take place and there were not 10,000, not 15,000, but our stewards said between 20 and 25,000 people. This meant that there had not been any kind of demonstration of this nature in Britain in the 30 years since the black community

John La Rose at the head of the Black Peoples Day of Action March, 2 March 1981.

had been living there, had arrived from the Caribbean. Ninety per cent of the people who marched were black and they marched through areas which previously had seen no marches. We crossed Blackfriars Bridge into the City. Blackfriars Bridge had not been crossed by a major demonstration since the Chartists in the 1830s. It marched down Fleet Street. It marched through the commercial centre of the city, Regent Street, parallel to Oxford Street, into Hyde Park. Not only that. but I, as the Chairman of the Committee, led a delegation to the Houses of Parliament where we met members of Parliament who had put on an early-day motion stating their opposition to what had taken place; and equally I went with that delegation to Downing Street and delivered a letter to Mrs Thatcher, the Prime Minister, also to Scotland Yard, and delivered a letter to David McNee, the Metropolitan Commissioner of Police. That delegation made it extremely clear to the British government that the demonstration of the black community and our allies in the country were totally dissatisfied with the way the Government had responded to what had taken place. For cynical reasons of state, a month after the New Cross Massacre, Thatcher and the Queen had sent messages of condolence to the victims of a fire in Ireland in the constituency of the then Prime Minister, Charles Haughey. And they said absolutely nothing of the holocaust in London, the capital city of the country. For us it was an act of barbarism.

You intend to make an International Commission of Inquiry?

Yes, the inquest into the fire took place over 4 weeks, lasting 13 days at the County Hall, in London, one of the biggest places where the inquest could have been held. The New Cross Massacre Parents Committee and the New Cross Massacre Action Committee were totally dissatisfied with the bias of the Coroner and the way he handled the inquest. We decided even before the Coroner's jury had handed out its verdict, that we would take legal action, if possible, to take out an injunction, to prevent the inquest from continuing. This went before a judge and he decided that seeing the inquest had gone on so far he would allow the inquest to continue, but he recognised that there had been gross irregularities during the inquest and, if we wished to come back for a new inquest, or about the inquest, we could do so.

After the Coroner's jury's verdict which was an open verdict, which meant that anybody could have done what happened, the Parents Committee and the New Cross Massacre Action Committee decided in the same week to do two things – first, to set up an International Commission of Inquiry and, second, to appeal against the verdict of the inquest. Now, a most unusual thing happened. The Attorney General gave his support, his authority, or fiat, to the request of the parents to have a new inquest. This has been unheard of in English jurisprudence for quite a long time – nobody remembers when an Attorney General in Britain has done something like that. That was given on May 11th of this year (1981). It meant that the government chief legal officer has supported parents' request before the Court of Appeal for a new inquest. Now the Court of Appeal will hear it soon we hope, after which we expect there will be a new inquest.[1] Despite that fact the New Cross Massacre Action Committee and the Parents Committee, (the Committee of the parents of the thirteen children who died) intend to go ahead with the International Commission of Inquiry in June of this year.[2]

Because of the way things are reported in the media, here in France people are much more aware of the riots which happened in Brixton in April and July 1981, and in other parts of the country, than they are of what happened in New Cross – where 13 people died whereas nobody died in the riots.

New Cross is an historic event in the history not only of the black community, but in the history of British society. Black struggles became centre stage in British politics, like the Irish struggles and the national struggle in Scotland, Ireland and Wales, as like the workers' struggles, especially those of the miners, against successive British governments. This has not happened before. Therefore it changed in an intrinsic manner the character of British politics. That's point number one. Number two is that the New Cross massacre campaign gave an enormous self-confidence to the black population in Britain – that has expressed itself politically, culturally, since 2nd March 1981. At Brixton, the youth who were fighting against the police in open insurrection, were saying, 'They burnt us out in New Cross we are burning them out now' and, after New Cross came Southall, and almost immediately after Southall came Toxteth, in Liverpool, and for the first time we saw a British Prime Minister, who is a person who is very accustomed and ready with words, in a state of speechlessness and perplexity. She did not know what to say or where to turn. The British establishment was in a state of perplexity because with that movement came the insurrections in about 60 cities.

Would you say that in these violent confrontations you see the profits of another conflict, the beginning of something new in British society, rather than the end of a movement which is now repressed?

That is the case. For example, the movement to which I belong, the Alliance of the Black Parents Movement, the Black Youth Movement, and the Race Today Collective, has taken part in London alone, in two important political actions involving the police, one in Notting Hill and the other in Hackney. Both were against the police authorities in those areas, two different areas of London, and had a vitality and energy of the kind which has not been seen in British society for quite some time. The Newton Rose case[3] and the case of the attack of the police on the Mangrove[4]...but, apart from these, there has been a recent outbreak of police disorder in St. Paul's, Bristol – where there had already been the first insurrection in 1980 – where the police were forced to leave the area for four hours without any kind of policing, and the result of that was that there is a parent of one of the persons involved, I think Mrs Nicholas is her name, who said (it was reported in the *Observer* newspaper 2 or 3 weeks ago) that 'Now there's no turning back – either one of us, or one of them, is going to be killed'. Now that's a new situation of parents and youth in unison against the police.

The riots in Toxteth, and the riots initiated by the black communities around the country were essentially against police repression and brutality about which the black community has been complaining for the last twenty years in Britain. There also were other factors, but these were not primary; they were secondary – unemployment, education, which resulted in unemployment, being unemployable and so on.

How does the black community view Lord Scarman's report on the activities of the police? How does the West Indian community participate in the British political system?

First, Lord Scarman's report. The black community has little confidence, no confidence, in what Scarman did. Scarman's history is that he did a silly report in Ireland before the outbreak of the IRA activities about 1969. That's not a very good record. Secondly the black community, on arriving in Britain in the 1950s, came as a result of an emigration that had suffered political defeat in the nationalist movement of the 1940s and 1950s. It was an emigration of workers who had fought in the national movement for independence. Many of them had belonged to the PNP – the People's National Party in Jamaica, the Peoples Progressive Party in Guyana, the West Indian Independence Party in Trinidad and Tobago, and other parties. Their presence in Britain meant that what they had fought for had not been realised and, as a result, they had come, as people come from all over Europe and the colonies to various Metropolitan centres; from North Africa to France, from Spain to France, from Turkey to Germany and from Yugoslavia to Germany, from the Caribbean to Britain, in the post-war economic development.

There was need for that labour and they came. But, because their presence in Britain always encountered hostility and neither of the parties were able to show they could control that hostility, could stand up to the hostility towards the emigration that came to Britain in the 1950s, neither of the parties (establishment parties, the Conservative Party and the Labour Party) were parties they could trust. And it has not been the habit of blacks ever since the 1950s to vote for either party –

Labour Party or Conservative Party. In other words, the black population has devoted its political skills to the mass struggles, rather than to the electoral struggles, and I would say that it is quite possible – I can't give

New Cross Massacre Inquest 13 Murdered No Cover Up

On Tuesday 21 April, 1981 the Inquest into the deaths of the 13 young blacks killed at the birthday party held at 439 New Cross Road on January 18th, begins.
The Coroner will decide the cause of their deaths. This he will do by assessing the evidence of various witnesses, of the police and their experts. The Coroner also selects the witnesses to be called. It is at this court that the police will officially present their case as to the cause of the fire and deaths.

WE KNOW that the police have ruled out racial motive. This they did the day after the fire and have been making statements to this effect ever since.

WE KNOW that the police line, according to the press reports, is that the fire started from within.

WE KNOW that the police have continuosly taken and spread the line that the party was a rowdy one where a fight or fights took place. They have tried to implicate various partygoers in this.

WE KNOW (according to The Guardian report of March 25th) that the police are saying that the person most able to help them to determine the circumstances which led to the fire, DIED in the fire.

WE KNOW that the police have put forward several theories which claim that the fire was started by accident.

WE KNOW that the national newspapers, television and radio have willingly publicised all these police claims as though they were fact.

WE KNOW that the police will try to cover up the real truth.

WE KNOW from previous experience not to trust the police investigation and to be constantly vigilant.

Despite their efforts the police have been unable to come up with a black scapegoat. And racial motive has not been seriously investigated.

At the Coroners Court they are likely to use all kinds of dirty tricks to bring forth evidence which will confuse the world as to the real nature of the party and the cause of the deaths. In this they will be willingly supported by the media and the Home Office.

It is vital that we picket and attend the Coroners Court. The police MUST not get away with the easy option of a verdict of accidental death or death by misadventure. Racial terror must be exposed and defeated.

Picket and attend the Coroners Court
County Hall London S.E.1.
From 9.30 a.m. to 1.00pm
Tuesday 21st April 1981
FOR THE WHOLE WEEK

Nearest tube stations: Waterloo or Westminster (walk over bridge).

Issued by the New Cross Massacre Action Committee, 74 Shakespeare Road, London SE24 OPT. Tel: 01-737 2268. Issued on April 3, 1981.

you any figures for this because I don't have them – it's quite possible that anything like 60 or 70% of the black population in Britain don't vote for either party.

What links are there between the community in the UK and the countries of origin?

The links? Let me put it differently – this emigration process is historically different from any other emigration from the Caribbean to any other part of the world. There were early emigrations to the Panama Canal and to Cuba. Those emigrations lost contact with their home base, did not return. They only went back with the international capitalist crisis in the 1930s and, as a result, participated in the workers' insurrections from 1935 to 1938. This emigration to Britain has been returning since the 1960s and its connection with its roots has been quite extraordinary. Reggae, certain kinds of speech patterns, all kinds of social customs and habits which one retains through one's relationship with one's country of origin, have been established as a result of that return of this emigration back to the Caribbean. In that sense it is historically different from any other emigration from the Caribbean.

Second point is that it is an emigration which arrived with a majority consciousness, not a minority consciousness as exists in the United States among the blacks. Because that majority was close itself to the struggle against the colonial system for political independence and social independence, in that sense again, it was different from any other emigration.

Thirdly, it became historically aware not simply of its relationship to the Caribbean, but to its past as part of the black consciousness and black power movement which developed around the world in the 1960s. With those features, it was, in many senses, an extraordinary emigration. In Britain, even today, the blacks behave as though they are a majority after a presence of 30 years in Britain where they are in fact a minority, because the sense of majority consciousness and its relationship to the black struggles in the world at the time of the Vietnam struggles, the black power struggles, African struggles for independence, still remains rooted in its consciousness and in its past. This makes it very different and carries with it a power which is unusual.

This immigration is starting to belong to English society today – so how do they organise this struggle for rights in English society?

Well, you see, in 1968, Powell made a statement – the famous 'rivers of blood' speech – Enoch Powell, MP, shadow Cabinet Minister. That became the moment of truth. Parents had illusions of return until that moment and they vested some of these illusions in their children. In effect, the nature of the economy means that as displaced labour, which is what they are, they cannot return to any kind of jobs except in a totally different political situation from what exists in the post-independence colonies in the Caribbean – neocolonialism in the Caribbean. They were forced into that realisation when Powell made this speech. And there was a very important conference organised by the independent black political movement, which had developed clearly in Britain around that moment, virtually a political movement of the youth – radical in consciousness, radical in perspective and radical in action – and they said, their slogan was 'Come what may, we are here to stay'. So that was the answer in 1968.

What about the children, the children of those people who came, who were born in Britain, how do they see their identity, their future, what are their dreams, what is it like to be young, black and British?
– and beautiful... What is it to be young, black and British? Well, first there are some sociologists who have a theory that they stand between two cultures. That is not true. The experience of that situation is that they stand within two cultures, two concentrics, not between, but within. This is a generation of youth who, by the age of 13, become totally absorbed in black music, totally absorbed in black identity, totally absorbed in black language and express themselves culturally every day, with their sound systems and with their institutions of entertainment which they organise themselves. They have had the problem of the education systems which programmes them for what they call 'shit jobs'. This they have rejected. In that sense they have affected the economic performance of the society, because their rejection of the 'shit jobs' meant that they were demanding for themselves reasonable jobs, decent jobs, like everybody else, properly paid, within the society which meant they were not a reserve army of labour of unemployed to be used against their parents and others in the labour market. Very important to remember that. Something historical I have never seen or heard of before. Secondly, they were absolutely convinced that British society was only Babylon and it was necessary not simply to get any reform, but to change it totally. The perspective therefore of the young in Britain is to mash up Babylon, to create a new society, where the social relations are not as barbaric as they are, that is something which is not humane, and make it more human.

We'd like to ask you now, what are the issues which create solidarity amongst the present day West Indian diaspora in the USA, France, the UK and Holland? If we take the example of a previous generation, Cesaire and Senghor came together on negritude. Where's the consensus now?

Well, for example, I came to live in London in 1961, as I told you, and that was the year that I made my first general contact. We had already made contact, in an abstract way in 1953 from Trinidad, where I came from, with Martinique and Guadeloupe. But the first genuine contact with the situation in Martinique, Guadeloupe and in Guyane was in 1961 because in that year we had the Organisation de la Jeunesse Anticolonialiste Martiniquaise (OJAM) and their proclamation of their determination to win independence. And there was a famous case here which involved those youths from Martinique in 1961. So, in a very concrete way from 1961 the movement, which had already almost formally gained independence in the anglophone Caribbean, made contact with that movement, which had developed in Martinique and Guadeloupe for independence.

I want you to answer, if you can, what is the difference between the black situation here in England and in France?

Well, it's very difficult... What I've just said is the first point. What I discovered was that the consciousness among West Indians from the anglophone Caribbean was a consciousness which had had its thrust since almost the end of the 19th century. There were two basic demands. One was for a better social life and power to the workers and the other was for political independence. That was part of the movement, ever since the end of the 19th century beginning of the 20th century, in the English-speaking Caribbean. It was surprising to us to find out that this did not appear to be the case in Martinique and Guadeloupe – though there were obviously signs that this was changing. Now what could be the difference is the history of French society, especially the French Revolution and its proclamation of 'Liberte, Egalite, Fraternite', as well as the declaration that the Blacks were free. Until the Napoleonic movement, which sought to crush the slave insurrections that had taken power in Guadeloupe, in Haiti – that led to an ambiguity in the situation, and that ambiguity remains in the relationship of those territories to France.

There was never any such ambiguity in the anglophone Caribbean with Britain. With regard to the United States, the connection is this. It is fairly obvious that the West Indian emigration to the United States always had a powerful impact on the consciousness of organisations of blacks in the United States. We can simply begin by referring to people like Edward Wilmot Blyden, Marcus Garvey, Stokely Carmichael and a whole host of people like that including Malcolm X, with a West Indian connection – a whole range of situations. The relationship to the black population had been there since the expansion of the slave-plantation culture, which had made certain the blacks in the Caribbean never did feel themselves a minority. The problem the slave-owners always had was, in the Caribbean, the fear of this black majority and it capacity for rebellion. That was their problem and the greatest strength. The West Indian emigration to the United States has always had that impact, and its connection has been of great importance. On the other hand, it must also be said that the activity of the blacks in the United States also had its impact on the blacks in the Caribbean especially in jazz and the cultural aspects; reggae has been influenced by jazz and popular culture in the United States. Reggae is an institution by itself, nevertheless it has been influenced by blues and so on. So it means that the connection, even though it has not been subjectively clear to its participants, that is to say the population of the United States and the Caribbean, at times, nevertheless has been objectively close.

The question was more about the blacks in England, their historical background analysed and the situation now, the difference between the black situation in England and France.

You see, I don't know the situation in France. I only know the situation in England and the United States. It's very obvious that I do know the situation in England. Let me answer that question. I'm always puzzled, despite my connection since 1961 with some of the youth who stood for independence, by the connection of the Martiniquais, Guadeloupean and Guyanese emigration to France. I'm puzzled about it because it has never been absolutely clear to me exactly what were the limits as well as the function, political function, of that emigration – either in relation to France, or in relation to the Caribbean. It has never been absolutely clear to me – partly because of the fact that it has been difficult for the majority consciousness that we cannot speak about and the thrust for political independence which traversed both the workers movement and then through the middle classes at a later period in the Caribbean – to understand what has happened in that relationship in

Martinique... So I've puzzled a lot about it. I've spoken to quite a few people on this subject – economists, sociologists – all kinds of people and I'm still very puzzled about it. I'm not absolutely clear what it means. I have no difficulty in understanding a relationship with the blacks in the United States and the blacks in Britain or the blacks in Holland. I have no difficulty. My difficulty is with the black immigration from Martinique and Guadeloupe and Guyane to France.

But it is clearer now, in Guadeloupe, in particular there is a rapidly growing movement for independence from France. That movement will affect the situation of blacks in France.

To come back to publishing – how important is the theme of migration in West Indian writing? And amongst the writers you edit, do you see a new generation of West Indian writers – I'm thinking of people like Linton Kwesi Johnson.

The population in the Caribbean, since the 16th, 17th, 18th centuries, is a population geared to emigration. That population was brought from Africa, seasoned in Barbados and exported from there to the south of the United States and to the north of the Caribbean, to Jamaica and so on, even after the abolition of slavery. There was an interesting study by a man called Roberts who showed how Barbados had become the place for the fertilization of the Caribbean population by the excess of labour which had been developed there in Barbados. So the West Indian population, ever since the 17th, 18th, 19th century, has been conditioned to emigration. Emigration is part of the consciousness of West Indians in that sense, in that clear sense.

Now what that does mean is that for the writer at first

there are no sources for the publishing of his work. You knew you had to emigrate to have it published or to emigrate your work to get it published, and most of the generation of West Indian writers in the anglophone Caribbean emigrated during the period of the 1950s to Britain and now some of them to the United States. So the theme of emigration is very important. But what has happened since in Britain is that there has been an explosion of cultural activity, especially in poetry, film and in plays, and that has taken place especially in the last five years or so.

Quite recently there was a black film festival in London, which was an enormous success, organised jointly with the Black Film Foundation in the United States and one was able to see the work – documentary work and feature film work – of the young, black, independent film-makers in Britain. The popular culture, reggae, has had again an enormous explosion, not only in Britain, but all over Europe. It is well-known, well-respected, well-loved, all over Europe, and, for example, a reggae poet like Linton Kwesi Johnson plays to audiences of 1,000 in London and plays also to similar audiences in different parts of Europe.

This population has become extremely confident, self-confident culturally. So you have the past, earlier writers, and the fact that they have emigrated but they have emigrated obviously with the basic West Indian culture from which they have written their work – people like Wilson Harris, Selvon, Salkey, Lamming, Naipaul and others. The theme of emigration appears in a number of their works, as it does in Austin Clarke, Edward Kamau Brathwaite and in young black writing in Britain.

How about the Rastafarian movement in Britain?
When people speak about the Rastafarian movement obviously they make, they lump, everything into one. Rastafarianism was never one movement – there are whole series and layers of movements. There has been social Rastafarianism, religious Rastafarianism, at least that and also, a popular Rastafarianism. When people lump Rastafarianism into one it's because they are not aware of the differences and the complexities in the situation as regards Rastafarianism. It's because Rastafarianism has these basic three areas which overlap – religious Rastafarianism, popular Rastafarianism and secular Rastafarianism – that's one of its strengths really. Now its impact has been this – the generation of the 1950s-1960s which became active in politics were part of the black power, black consciousness movement – Afros, 'black is beautiful', all that – this new generation, the younger generation, self-confident, full of thrust, they tend in the majority to be Rastafarians, either religious, which is the minority, secular or popular. I make the difference between secular and religious – the two are closest to each other; if you are a religious Rastafarian you will find yourself closest to the person who is a secular Rastafarian, who has some belief; and then there's the person who is a popular Rastafarian who just says that he is a Rastafarian, he has his hair, he buys the posters, and things of that sort and he thinks it significant because he is against Babylon.

How do you see the role of the 'emigre' intellectual in the immigrant community in British society, like you, and your friend, James, who wrote *The Black Jacobins*?

CLR James is now 82 and he has been living in the Caribbean for many years and teaching in the United States. But recently all his works have been reprinted in Britain and he has given a number of lectures and the importance of James is that he thinks in a radical, unique Marxist perspective. His influence on Caribbean life, on Caribbean intellectual life as well as on life among the people of Caribbean origin in Britain, and more important at this moment, is that it has affected a search for a new radicalism in Britain. His lectures, his talks, his radio and television appearances had wide audiences. James will be at the opening of the Book Fair which will take place from the 1st to the 3rd of April 1982 – he is not an active person. He was active in the 1930s, he was active in the 1960s but he is not active any more. His influence is intellectual.

With people like myself, it's entirely different. I have lived in England for 20 years. I am now in my 50s and during those 20 years of active political, cultural and social life in Britain I have been part of and I've affected and influenced the political, social and cultural movement of blacks, to the point where it is at the present moment. So my position is entirely different from James', because of the fact that I am still active in the politics of blacks in Britain. Our relationship to the mass of the population is that there is a clear position in Britain at the present moment.

The British State finds it necessary, like they did in the 1940s and 1950s in the Caribbean, to create a black intermediary class to stand between the black unemployed and the black working class and to collaborate with the state against the radical perspective and radical and revolutionary struggles of the black working class and unemployed. There is a titanic battle which is being waged between these two perspectives in the black community.

The organisation to which belong makes its position absolutely clear. The Alliance of the Black Parents Movement, the Black Youth Movement and the Race Today Collective – we are part of the perspective of struggle to change British society – it is part of the working class, the black working class and unemployed perspective in Britain, and we are in opposition to the black middle classes whose function is to police that black working class – act as intermediaries for the state. The black middle class has failed signally so far because its social base is weak, not like the population of Indian and Pakistan, and Bangladeshi origin the social base among the middle classes in Britain. They are much stronger economically, socially and religiously because if you are a Muslim, you have the Mosque, if you are a Hindu there is a temple and if you miss either of these, there is the business, and that middle class is powerful and strong. The struggle within the Asian communities, as they are called in Britain at the moment (the community of Bangladeshi, Indians and Pakistanis, and people of Bangladeshi, Pakistani and Indian origin), is between the youth and unemployed and working class – this section of the black working class, which showed itself at Grunwick, Imperial Typewriters and other major historic struggles in Britain which they themselves have waged in the last decade – and the position and perspective of that middle class element that I've just described to you in that part of society.

Our perspective says very clearly that Britain is a society of nationalities and ethnic communities: English, Scots, Welsh, Irish nationalities as well as the West Indian, Asian, and other ethnic communities.

Inside both the nationalities as well as the ethnic communities there's a fierce internal class battle raging in Britain. We stand for a horizontal alliance across classes to change British society. That's our perspective. It's clear as a political perspective. We always knew, because of our experience of the struggle, revolutionary nationalism and conservative nationalism in the Caribbean, that there would emerge inside Scottish nationalism, inside Welsh nationalism, inside Irish nationalism, a struggle for revolutionary, social change and a struggle for conservative maintenance of the status quo. And that has already occurred inside Scottish nationalism, inside Irish nationalism, inside Welsh nationalism. The evidence is absolutely clear there. We stand with those sections for change in British society and obviously it's a multinational state, a multi-ethnic state. One thinks of the Soviet Union as a multi-national state. You don't think of other European states as multiethnic and multi-national states, but so too is Holland, so too is Belgium, see what I mean? These are... and so too is France, isn't it? These are multinational, multi-ethnic states, where certain sections have dominated other sections and centralised the power in their hands and that is the state. The English did it in the British state and other people did it in other states in Europe. There's the Russification of the Soviet Union under the Russian domination, cultural as well as economic and social.

Does the image of West Indian society portrayed in V.S. Naipaul's novel, *Guerillas* seem to you accurate?
Naipaul is a major novelist, a major talented novelist, along with people like Lamming, and especially the most significant of them all, Wilson Harris. It is

important for me to say something in connection with Naipaul. I have never thought that there was something separating Britain and colony. It was one economy. Britain and the Empire was one economy and therefore one history with different parts. Now, there's a man called F.R. Leavis, a famous and well-known English critic, who speaks about the great tradition in the English novel. It's a very important book, it's a very important work written by Leavis and I have a great admiration for this criticism. My view of Naipaul is that Naipaul at this historical moment, is in that great tradition of the English novel, at the fag end of the empire. That tradition will end at some historical moment and that sensibility which Naipaul expresses so well because of his talents, that sensibility of self-contempt, which is part of the heritage of the colonised is part of that very tradition of the bourgeois English novel ending with the themes of the demise of the Empire.

How would you sum up your experience in the UK?
My experiences of the UK? I did not intend when I went to the UK to stay more than three years. I intended to study law. I broke with it almost in the first year of my being there. It's an illusion which broke with that you could study law and return to work in the Caribbean. I pursued my original my most serious interests which were cultural and political, music, literature, politics, which resulted in the publishing house I established and the other work we have done in Britain and in the Caribbean because it's a perspective which takes in my interest and work in both areas. It's also extended beyond that in Britain, in Africa, Afro-America. Now, finally, what I wish to say about that is I always realised

the extent to which the distance you have from your past focusses attention more seriously on it. Many writers have had that – there is Lawrence and others. I have found that in my separation from the Caribbean, I have understood the Caribbean better and myself better and have been able to contribute to the situation in the Caribbean and to the situation in Britain much better. I have the closest relationship with the struggles in the Caribbean and with the struggles in Britain and that relationship I think to be an important part of the international perspective which I share with others in my work.

NOTES:

1. The application for a new inquest was refused on 8th July 1982 by Lord Chief Justice Lane who said in the High Court that the coroners jury could not have returned anything but an open verdict in the circumstances.
2. The New Cross Massacre Action Committee intends to hold the international commission of inquiry in 1983.
3. Newton Rose, a black Londoner convicted in December 1981 of the murder of a National Front supporter won a final ruling in the House of Lords in July 1982 that he had been wrongfully convicted. Unanimously the Lords dismissed an appeal by the prosecution for a retrial. In the original trial, the Judge had committed a 'material irregularity' by sending an improper message to the jury of ten whites and two blacks (which convicted Rose by a 10 – 2 majority) that if they did not complete their deliberations in 15 minutes they would be discharged.
4. On Christmas Eve 1981, over 50 police officers raided the Mangrove, a restaurant in All Saints Road (Notting Hill, London) used as a meeting place for black people. The area was sealed off, and according to Scotland Yard, up to 200 or more police may have been held in reserve.

DEFEATS AND ADVANCES

EPILOGUE BY GUS JOHN
APRIL 2011

The New Cross Fire marred the lives of the families of the fourteen young people who perished as a result of the fire and of the survivors, many of whom carry the physical and mental scars to this day. In the years that followed, however, they have been supported by the struggle for justice and against racism and fascism which was pursued with unprecedented vigour by black communities up and down the country.

No one could fully imagine, then or now, the anguish and loss felt by the families and the recurring nightmares of the survivors. However, the fact that communities across the nation identified with their pain and loss and saw the tragedy as a catalyst for an onslaught on racism in British society and its institutions, made it possible for the families and survivors alike not to be seen as victims but as people actively engaged in seeking justice for their loved ones and themselves and demanding change in the way the society treats us because we are black.

And change was not long in coming.

Such change soon became evident in, among others, the following five areas.

First, coping with bereavement.

Most of the thirteen young people whose lives the fire claimed on the night had been barely left school. Some were at college and all were part of vibrant youth networks in their families and communities. Those

Black Peoples Day of Action March passing through Elephant and Castle, 2 March 1981.

bereaved were therefore not just their immediate families but their extended community of school and college friends, youths in their peer group and a host of significant individuals in their lives, all of whom were potentially vulnerable to the impact of grief and sudden loss.

A number of individuals, church leaders and ministers of religion, psychiatrists and psychologists, counsellors and therapists spontaneously offered their services and organised themselves to provide bereavement counselling for as many as possible of those impacted upon by the tragedy. The need for sustained bereaved support was underscored by the death of the fourteenth victim of the fire, a traumatised survivor who jumped to his death from the block of flats where he lived.

Thus was established the practice of offering bereavement counselling to families and others affected by incidents involving sudden death within communities across the country.

Second, part of the police response to the New Cross Fire was the arrest of young people who had been at the party, forcing some of them to sign statements which supported the theory the police sought to prove, for example, that the fire had been caused by a fight between young people on the ground floor of the house.

Drawing upon the experience of organising the legal defence of young black men framed or wrongfully arrested by the police, members of the New Cross Massacre Action Committee monitored police arrests and detention, took statements from those bailed by the police, ensured that lawyers kept them at the centre of the preparation of their defence and that the police knew that the community would not sit by and allow them to criminalise the party goers who had themselves been traumatised by the fire.

That practice of keeping defendants at the centre of their legal defence and making sure lawyers did not sideline them and in some cases make deals with the police and simply present defendants with a 'fait accompli' enabled the New Cross Massacre Action Committee to expose the tactics of the police and give the young people the confidence to stand up to them. Furthermore, it radicalised a good number of solicitors and barristers and gave them an understanding of the political context within which the police operated routinely to oppress young black people and deny them their civil liberties, the context in which they themselves needed to operate as advocates.

On 11 April 1981, one month after the New Cross Massacre Black People's Day of Action, there was a mass uprising in Brixton as a direct result of provocative, saturation policing and targeting of black young people using 'Stop and Search' powers, which the local Commander of Police called 'Operation Swamp '81'. The Brixton Defence Committee was formed not only to provide guidance and legal support to those arrested, but to monitor the actions of the police and ensure that people were not targeted indiscriminately and denied their rights. It operated according to the same principles and employed similar methods to those which were even then being applied in the case of the black young people who had been targeted by the police in the ongoing New Cross Fire investigation. As the mass uprisings spread across Britain's inner cities that Summer, defence committees sprung up in Manchester, Liverpool, Birmingham and other parts of London, each of them organised on the model of the New Cross Massacre Action Committee's intervention in New Cross.

Third, for at least two decades prior to the New Cross Massacre, African and Asian communities in Britain had experienced racist attacks and murders by individuals acting alone or as part of organised fascist groups such as the National Front, Column 88 and the British Movement. Local and national news media occasionally carried reports of such attacks. The Black and Asian press were typically the media that carried reports of such violations of black people and their fundamental human rights. Reports to the police were often not followed up and when they were, they were pursued as crimes against the person or criminal damage to property but not as racially motivated or race hate crimes.

In 1977, the Joint Committee Against Racialism (JCAR) was formed. By 1981, following the New Cross Massacre, JCAR was able to present the Home Office with a dossier detailing over 11,000 racist attacks. In 1981 alone, 26 racist murders were recorded as compared with a total of 28 over the previous ten years. William Whitelaw, then Conservative Home Secretary, set up a Home Office inquiry into racial attacks. The 1981 Home Office inquiry recommended:

- Police forces to collect data on racial attacks
- Reporting of racial incidents to be immediate
- Liaison arrangements to be explored by police, local authorities and community groups (the Police Community Liaison arrangements that involved the police, Lambeth Council and the Brixton community had broken down some time prior to the uprisings, principally because of the community's protest at the way policing was done)

- Ethnic minorities to assist in training of police

As Professor Benjamin Bowling wrote in *Violent Racism – Victimisation, Policing and Social Context* (1998):

> Until (1981), as the problem did not exist, there was no publicly stated police or government policy to deal with it. Within two years violent racism had the status of urgent priority.

In fact, it was not until the Crime and Disorder Act came into force in September 1998 that a number of specific offences of racially aggravated crime were created, based on offences of wounding, assault, damage, harassment and threatening/abusive behaviour. The monitoring of reported racial incidents that followed the Home Office inquiry report of 1981 had indicated that these types of crime were those most commonly experienced by victims of racial violence or harassment.

Fourth, following the Brixton uprisings in April 1981, the Scarman Inquiry recommended, among other things, that the police take steps to recruit more black officers.

John Lea, writing about 'the Politics of Policing' in 2007, stated:

> In London almost 25 per cent of the population is of non-white ethnicity. When Lord Scarman reported on the Brixton riots in 1981 black officers constituted merely 0.5 percent of the Metropolitan Police. He called for a substantial increase in the number of non-white officers. But progress has been slow. By 2001 a little over 4 per cent of Metropolitan Police officers were from a minority ethnic background. At

the end the of the financial year 2003/4 it was 6.6 per cent. The Home Office has set a target of 25.9 percent ethnic minority officers by 2009. Many consider this unlikely to be achieved.

(http://www.bunker8.pwp.blueyonder.co.uk/cjs/26902.htm)

The Home Office target was in direct response to one of the findings of the Stephen Lawrence Inquiry (1999) into the racist murder of Stephen Lawrence in 1993, i.e., that the Metropolitan Police was 'institutionally racist', a finding which was prompted by the evidence the Inquiry received from the Met's Black Police Association which was formed in 1994.

The widespread criticism in black communities of the police investigation into the New Cross Fire and especially of their treatment of the young black party goers, the police conduct during the Black People's Day

John La Rose with members of the bereaved families on the First Anniversary of the New Cross Massacre Fire.

of Action and the nature of the police operation that led to the Brixton uprising shone the spotlight on black officers in the Metropolitan Police. They began to associate much more directly their own experience of racism in the police service with the way the communities to which they belonged experienced policing in London and elsewhere. Throughout the 1980s, black police officers became increasingly conscious that they were part of an arm of the State that was targeting black people disproportionately through 'Stop and Search', the Sus laws, and raids on places of entertainment and on residences, at a time when the economy was in decline and unemployment was affecting black youth more than any other section of the population.

For example, Superintendent Paul Wilson speaking at a conference on 'rank and file participation in police reform' in October 2006 about 'the development and role of a Black Police Association' noted that when Brixton erupted in 1981, whereas unemployment in Brixton stood at 13% overall, among ethnic minorities it was 25.4% and among black youths nationwide it was estimated at between 55% and 60%. It was precisely that group, displaced from the labour market in such high numbers, that bore the brunt of police oppression in cities such as London, Bristol, Birmingham, Leeds Liverpool and Manchester. It was they, too, that black police officers, often working with their white colleagues, were frequently confronting on the streets.

Black police officers drew strength from the political struggles in their own communities to confront the racism they were experiencing in the police service. It is their identification with that resistance in communities, invariably led by young people however spontaneously, that gave rise eventually to the formation of the Black Police Association in the Metropolitan Police Service in 1994. By 1999, when the Home Office framed its plan of action in response to the Stephen Lawrence Inquiry's findings and recommendations, it was mandating chief constables in the 43 police forces in England and Wales to support the development and work of Black Police Associations among their black officers and civilian staff.

Scarman also recommended that active steps be taken to create a black middle class so that black people could be seen to be represented in the professions and in the mainstream of British society. Therefore, in 1981 the government issued a circular encouraging local authorities to set up special access courses for black adults to provide them with alternative entry qualifications for further and higher education to train for a career in the caring professions. Thus were laid the foundations for a rapid increase in the number of black social workers, probation officers, careers officers and the like. Local government was also cajoled to draw up and operate equal opportunity policies and take action to increase the number of black workers they employed.

Fifth, black members of parliament.

Throughout the 1970s, there was a debate within the trade union movement and in the Labour Party at local level about the need for autonomous black political organisation within their ranks. This debate was fuelled by the widespread evidence of trade unions failing to acknowledge the extent of racial discrimination among their white membership and to properly represent black members who brought complaints of racial discrimination. By 1981 and the New Cross Massacre and Day of Action, communities generally and black members of the Labour Party in particular were challenging not just trade unions, but Labour run councils and the Labour Party at national level about their record in defending the rights of black people and combating racism in their employment practices, service delivery and selection procedures governing both local and national representation. This, it must be remembered, was a period when it was taken for granted that the Labour Party could depend on the black vote in local and general elections.

The Labour Party Black Sections movement grew out of that community agitation and by 1983 was able to table a demand for greater representation at the Labour Party conference. Four years later, four Black Sections members, Bernie Grant, Diane Abbott, Paul Boateng and Keith Vaz were elected to Parliament as Britain's first post-war black MPs.

Marc Wadsworth, himself an original Black Sections member, writing in the Guardian in October 2008 to mark the 25th anniversary of Black Sections stated:

> None of the movement's achievements would have been possible without protest and agitation. The uprisings that occurred in the early 1980s in Brixton, Bristol, Birmingham, Leeds, Manchester, Liverpool and elsewhere acted as a wake-up call to a society that was either indifferent or hostile to the demands of disenfranchised and disadvantaged black people. But the legitimate calls for fair representation made by black communities whose electoral support was given overwhelmingly to Labour were stubbornly resisted by the party leadership of Neil Kinnock and Roy Hattersley, who were obsessed with defeating a rising left-wing rank and file.

Despite this opposition, Black Sections won. We achieved a 500-fold increase in African-Caribbean and Asian representation in town halls around the country, four black council leaders, four black MPs, and Bill Morris as the first black trade union general secretary. On top of that, black self-organised groups were formed in trade unions and even by police officers. And the TUC created places on its general council and executive for black representatives.

The New Cross Massacre Black People's Day of Action was both the application of a process of self organisation on a massive scale and an unleashing of people's power and self assertiveness that impacted upon even the most resistant institutions in the society. The tried and tested principles and method of organisation that the late John La Rose as Chair of the New Cross Massacre Action Committee and others from the movement he led brought to the community's response to the massacre laid the foundations for sustained action by the mass of unemployed black youths, by black police officers, by Labour Party supporters and many other sections of the black community.

The horror of the New Cross Massacre, compounded by the crass and incompetent response of the State (prime minister, police investigation, coroner) will undoubtedly be a memory the survivors and relatives cannot erase. The political advances the massacre spurred and the momentous contribution to change in British society and to the self empowerment of black people that the response to the tragedy triggered will hopefully remain lasting monuments to the memory of those who perished.

13 OF OUR
CHILDREN
MURDERED
JAN '81
ANDREW GOODING
OWEN THOMPSON

APPENDICES

Opposite: *439 New Cross Road, scene of the fire.*

NEW CROSS MASSACRE 1981

Roseline Henry Born 23 September 1964	Died 18 January 1981
Patricia Johnson Born 16 May 1965	Died 18 January 1981
Humphrey Brown Born 4 July 1962	Died 18 January 1981
Gerry Paul Francis Born 21 August 1963	Died 18 January 1981
Owen Wesley Thompson Born 11 September 1964	Died 18 January 1981
Andrew Gooding Born 18 February 1962	Died 18 January 1981
Peter Campbell Born 23 February 1962	Died 18 January 1981
Yvonne Ruddock Born 17 January 1965	Died 24 January 1981
Glenton Powell Born 18 January 1966	Died 25 January 1981
Lloyd Hall Born 28 November 1960	Died 18 January 1981
Patrick Cummings Born 21 September 1964	Died 18 January 1981
Paul Ruddock Born 19 November 1960	Died 9 February 1981
Steve Collins Born 2 May 1963	Died 18 January 1981

Anthony Berbeck Born August 17 1962, died on 9th July 1983 after falling from the balcony of a block of council flats in South London, He was at the party and became mentally disturbed following the death of his best friends. He was the 14th victim of the fire.

DECLARATION OF NEW CROSS

Made At The New Cross Massacre Black People's Day of Action On Monday, 2nd March, 1981.

1. On Sunday, 18th January, 1981 in an unparalleled act of savagery, thirteen (13) young people, aged from fourteen (14) to twenty-two (22), were murdered at 439 New Cross Road, in the heart of London, capital city of Britain. They were attending a birthday party. They were black.

2. The national authorities in Parliament and Government, in a further act of barbarism, ignored the tragedy of the families of the dead and injured. But they sent messages of condolence to the fire victims in Ireland, for cynical reasons of state.

3. The authorities have ignored for three decades the pain, the rage and outrage of the black communities around the country at the racial murders, injuries and threats to our existence. Threats have come even from the highest authorities in the land.

4. The New Cross Massacre Black People's Day of Action is another stage in the response of the black people and of our allies in the country to this savagery and this barbarism.

5. We warn the country and the world that there will be no social peace while blacks are attacked, killed, injured and maimed with impunity on the streets or in our homes.

LETTERS DELIVERED

to the Prime Minister, the Commissioner of the Metropolitan Police and the speaker of The House of Commons on Monday 2nd March, 1981, The New Cross Massacre Black People's Day of Action, by the New Cross Massacre Action Committee's delegation.

The Prime Minister
10 Downing Street,
London SW1

Dear Prime Minister,

The New Cross Massacre Action Committee has delegated us to protest at the failure of your government to reflect the outrage and deep feelings of the black community at the murder of thirteen (13) young blacks at 439 New Cross Road on Sunday 18th January, 1981.

We note that you wrote, not to the parents themselves, but to Sybil Phoenix a full five weeks after the events. This we take as a serious and calculated insult.

We enclose for your information the Declaration of New Cross 1981.

Yours sincerely,

John La Rose
Chairman

The Commissioner of Police,
New Scotland Yard,
8–10 Broadway,
London SW1

Dear Commissioner,

The New Cross Massacre Action Committee has delegated us to protest at the failure of your police force to understand the outrage and deep feelings of the black community at the murder of thirteen (13) young blacks at 439 New Cross Road on Sunday 18th January, 1981.

We note that after six (6) weeks no one has yet been found responsible for the murder of the 13 young blacks and racial motive is generally discounted. The New Cross Massacre Action Committee express our uneasiness and dissatisfaction with the state of investigation and hope that no black scapegoat will be made to answer the murder charge.

We enclose for your in formation the Declaration of New Cross 1981.

Yours sincerely,
John La Rose Chairman

The Speaker,
House of Commons
Westminster,
London SW1

Dear Speaker,

The New Cross Massacre Action Committee has delegated us to protest at the failure of the House of Commons to reflect the outrage and deep feelings of the black community at the murder of thirteen (13) young blacks at 439 New Cross Road on Sunday 18th January, 1981.

We note with regret that it was not until a delegation from the New Cross Massacre Action Committee saw members of the House of Commons on Wednesday February 25th that any action was taken in Parliament. We therefore ask you to note and bring to the attention of the House our profound dissatisfaction with this situation.

We enclose for your information the Declaration of New Cross 1981.

Yours sincerely,
John La Rose Chairman

cc. Mr Christopher Price MP
Mr John Silkin MP
Mr John Tilley MP
Mr Reg Race MP
Mr Frank Dobson MP

EARLY DAY MOTION

Notice of Motions for which no days have been fixed

TRAGEDY IN NEW CROSS
Mr Michael Foot
Mr Denis Healey
Mr Frederick Willey
Mr Michael Cocks
Mr John Silkin
Mr Roy Hattersley

Guy Barnett
That this house expresses its sympathy with, and condolences to, the friends and relatives of those who died or were injured in the fire at 439 New Cross Road, on Sunday 18th January.

As an Amendment to Mr Michael Foot's proposed Motion (Tragedy in New Cross):
Mr Christopher Price
Mr John Tilley
Mr Frank Dobson
Mr Alfred Dubs
Mr Reg Race
Jo Richardson

Line 3, at end add
'and calls upon the police to conclude their enquiries as rapidly as possible; deplores the attacks on the black community by racially motivated groups, such as the National Front, the British Movement and Column 88; and declares its determination to ensure there shall be equality of rights and esteem for all citizens regardless of race or colour'.

PRESS STATEMENT

The New Cross Massacre Action Committee condemns the confusion which the *Daily Mail* has deliberately sought to create by publishing its story in today's issue with the heading 'Killer Blaze Charge Soon'.

Scotland Yard Press Office said tonight that this story is 'completely untrue'. They also said that the young blacks who were in Lewisham Police Station were not under arrest. 'They were purely witnesses who were corroborating statements already given. They were at the party and were in the police station to give statements .' Asked if they had been released, Scotland Yard said: 'They were never under arrest'.

The New Cross Massacre Action Committee has warned the entire public that the police are likely to arrest some blacks on the eve of the Black People's Day of Action on Monday 2nd March to divert attention from the Demonstration and weaken the Day of Action. The *Daily Mail* story and the ITN news today have served that purpose.

A delegation from the New Cross Massacre Action Committee and Mrs Ruddock, who lost two of her children among the 13 blacks murdered on Sunday January 18th, met MPs at the House of Commons at 3.15pm today. The delegation met Mr John Silkin, Shadow Leader of the House, Mr Christopher Price MP, Mr Frank Dobson MP, Mr Reg Race MP, and Mr John Tilley MP.

The delegation requested that Parliament adjourn for the day as a mark of respect for the 13 young blacks who died in New Cross on 18th January. This was done in the case of the fire in Ireland recently.

The delegation also requested that if this could not be

done, that Parliament should adjourn for a few hours while the Demonstration of the Black People's Day of Action is in the vicinity of Parliament. The MPs agreed to put down an 'Early Day Motion' condemning racist attacks on the black population on Monday 2nd March.

The MPs were asked to specifically mention National Front, Column 88 and the British Movement in the motion in keeping with the discussion that had taken place between the delegations. Mr John Silkin also said that the motion would be put down for debate with the support of Labour MPs.

The delegation also visited the Jamaican High Commission and received very sympathetic attention from the High Commissioner, Mr Peart. He was asked if he would close the High Commission on the Black People's Day of Action. He said the High Commission would show their sympathy on the day by closing for a few hours.

Issued at 7.30pm on Wednesday 25th February 1981.
Given to Press Association at 8.40pm.

NEW CROSS MASSACRE MASSIVE POLICE AND LEGAL COVER UP

The Parents, Relatives and New Cross Massacre Action Committee Fight On

On July 8th, Lord Chief Justice Lane, Lord Justice Watkins and Mr Justice Robert Goff refused to quash the open verdict given by the jury at the inquest on the New Cross Fire in April/May 1981. They also refused to grant a new Inquest. The New Cross Massacre took place on January 18th, 1981 at 439 New Cross Road, London SE14. 13 young black people died and 27 were injured.

The parents and widow of the dead stated in their legal action challenging the inquest verdict:

a. That given that forensic evidence pointed to the fire being deliberately caused the Coroner misdirected the jury as to the facts, and verdicts open to them.
b. The Coroner adopted the theory of the fight as causing the fire against all other possible theories of the fire.
c. The Coroner failed to keep written notes of the proceedings as required by Rule 30 of the Coroner's Rules 1953.
d. The Coroner did not sum up properly, he read from witness statements taken by the police.
e. In summing up the Coroner omitted matters said in evidence while including other things which witnesses had not said when they gave their evidence.

The parents and their legal representatives were dissatisfied with the Inquest even before it ended. They had gone before Mr Justice Comyn at the High Court seeking an injunction to stop the Inquest. When he heard of the failure of the Coroner, Dr Arthur Gordon

Davies to take notes he expressed the view that this was a grave irregularity, and if the parents were dissatisfied with the verdict they should return to him.

After the Inquest the parents decided to appeal against the Open Verdict.

The Attorney General, Sir Michael Havers, gave his backing to the parents Appeal to quash the verdict and their application for a new inquest.

When the parents returned to Justice Comyn for leave to appeal he granted their application but questioned whether a new Inquest would not open old wounds.

The parents immediately wrote to the Lord Chancellor making it clear that they wanted a new Inquest and that the old wounds would continue to fester until they were granted one.

They also drew the attention of the Lord Chancellor to the fact that the Coroner had allowed the police to tape the proceedings without their knowledge or any consultation with them or their legal representatives.

The Appeal 5th – 8th July, 1982

The judges refused to accept any single point made by the families. They systematically put the lid on any legal come back. In a most brutal judgement they exonerated the Coroner, they even said he acted commendably. This shows the extent to which the authorities are prepared to go to cover up the massacre at 439 New Cross Road.

Lord Justice Lane, Lord Justice Watkins and Mr Justice Goff ruled that any irregularities or errors in the Coroner's behaviour were not serious enough to merit the quashing of the Inquest verdict and further stated that given the hostility of the families and their supporters at the Inquest it was surprising that he did not make more mistakes. They launched an attack on the parents' lawyers (Michael Mansfield, Ian McDonald and Rock Tansey) for not assisting the Coroner in the conduct of his biased inquest.

The police led by Commander Stockwell, the media, and the Coroner had tried to convince everybody before and during the Inquest that the fire was caused by a fight between black youths in the front room of 439 New Cross Road. Now, at the Appeal, Lord Justice Lane described the fight theory as 'irrelevant' and the Coroner's DC Henry Brookes called it 'a wicked shame'. So having dismissed the main thrust of the Inquest put forward by the police over 13 days, the judges nevertheless found the Inquest satisfactory

The Coroner's conduct of the Inquest from April 21st to May 13th 1981, was universally condemned as biased and incompetent

The judgement o the Court of Appeal endorses the police cover up and corruption which has now gone on for 18 months.

It is the police and Coroner who chose the witnesses at the Inquest. The police took over 1,000 statements. They picked 65 witnesses to suit their own theory. There were other witnesses who could have been called and who would have assisted a genuinely conducted Inquest aimed at finding the truth. The Inquest was to be their political reply to the mass mobilisation of the black community and the New Cross Massacre Action Committee's Black Peoples Day of Action on March 2nd, 1981.

Commander Stockwell then leading the investigation in May 1981 said that he had 50 policemen at his disposal since January 20, 1981 and had spent £320,000 of tax payers money up to the Inquest. At the Inquest

Vigil outside the Royal Courts of Justice on the First Anniversary of the New Cross Massacre Fire, 18 January 1982.

Photos: Julian Stapleton

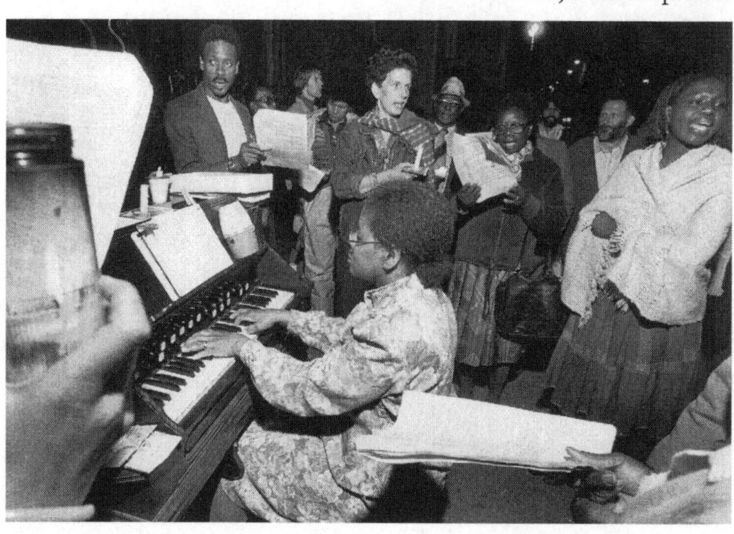

Stockwell said he had 20 other people to interview. Since the Inquest the Inquiry came under Commander Phelan and Det. Supt. Bell they have come up with nothing, 'no new fresh evidence'.

At the end of the day the parents have nothing from the police nothing from the Coroner's Inquest and nothing from the Judges in the High Court – it is the most massive police and legal cover up.

The New Cross Massacre Action Committee, together with the relatives of the 13 dead young people do not intend to let this matter rest. We do not intend to forget that in addition to the 13 dead, 27 young blacks suffered serious injuries. The judges' ruling has not weakened our resolve nor the resolve of the parents and relatives. It has confirmed the extent to which the people who hold power in this country will go to cover up the New Cross Massacre.

The parents and the New Cross Massacre Action Committee said on May 13, 1981 the day of the Inquest verdict, that they rejected the open verdict of the Inquest and would hold an International Commission of Inquiry into the New Cross Massacre. This is the next step. Commissioners from Africa, Caribbean, India, USA, Europe, and Britain have already confirmed their willingness to participate in such a Commission. We call on all organisations and individuals who feel outraged at the decision of the High Court on the Appeal to continue to support the New Cross parents, their relatives and the New Cross Massacre Action Committee.

13 DEAD NOTHING SAID. COULD WE FORGET. WE WILL NOT FORGET

extract from 1991 brochure
10th International Book Fair of
Radical Black and Third World Books

The lives of 13 black youth, all between the ages of 15 and 20 years old, were snuffed out on Sunday 18th January 1981 by a racist firebomb at 439 New Cross Road. They were enjoying themselves at Yvonne Ruddock's 16th birthday party; the next moment they were dead. Both Yvonne and her elder brother Paul Ruddock died in the fire. 27 people were badly injured. The parents, families and friends of the dead and injured were devastated.

This was the peak of the racial attacks and racial murders experienced by the black population since our coming to Britain. The response in the black communities was instant and enraged. On Tuesday January 20th 1981, just two days after the fire, over 300 people, from the Midlands to London, formed the New Cross Massacre Action Committee. On Sunday 25 January 1981, the Sunday following the massacre, a public meeting of around 2000 people took place at the Moon Shot Club (Pagnell Street Centre) in Lewisham followed by a demonstration to 439 New Cross Road, where the fire and massacre of the black youth had taken place. The militant demonstration stayed in front of the house and blocked the A2, the major road leading into and out of London, for several hours.

The New Cross Massacre Action Committee, meeting on Tuesday January 27th, decided to hold the Black Peoples Day of Action on Monday March 2nd 1981 to

MEETING SATURDAY 2ND MARCH 1991

10TH ANNIVERSARY NEW CROSS MASSACRE

BLACK PEOPLES DAY OF ACTION

MARCH 2ND 1981 - MARCH 2ND 1991

On Sunday 18th January 1981, thirteen (13) young blacks, nearly all school students and teenagers, were burnt to death in a firebomb attack on the home of the Ruddock family at 439 New Cross Road, New Cross, London SE14.

SPEAKERS

New Cross Parents

Dr. Aggrey Burke - Families Support Group

Darcus Howe - Vice Chairman of the New Cross Fire Fund & Vice Chairman of **the New Cross Massacre Action Committee**

Ali Hussein - New Cross Massacre Action Committee, North East

Gus John - New Cross Massacre Action Committee, North West

Linton Kwesi Johnson - New Cross Massacre Action Committee

John La Rose - Chairman of the New Cross Massacre Action Committee & **Secretary/Treasurer of the New Cross Fire Fund**

Ian Macdonald Q.C. - Appeared for the parents at the Coroner's Inquest

Michael Mansfield Q.C. - Appeared for the parents at the Coroner's Inquest

Alex Pascall - Chairman of the New Cross Fire Fund

Bishop Wilfred Wood - Provided religious solace for the parents and conducted funeral services

Gospel Singers

Chair: Roxy Harris - New Cross Massacre Action Committee

All the speakers were involved with and active participants in this historic moment

at: BRIXTON VILLAGE (formerly St. Matthews Meeting Place)
Brixton Hill, London SW2
at 7.00pm
on Saturday March 2nd 1991
nearest tube station - Brixton (Victoria line)

Issued by the 10th Anniversary New Cross Massacre Action Committee
c/o 76 Stroud Green Road, London N4 3EN. Tel: 071-272 4889

protest against the racial massacre, the indifference of the government and media, and the inadequacy and bias of the police investigation. The Committee chose Monday for the demonstration to create maximum impact on a working day and to bring maximum pressure on the government and society. The NCMAC met in preparation week after week in the Black Peoples Assembly, in open discussion and, then right after, in working and planning sessions. Public meetings were held all over Britain to inform the black communities of the details of the massacre and to mobilise them for the Black Peoples Day of Action. Leaflets were printed by the NCMAC and copies were made and distributed by members of the black communities quite independently so as to support the Black Peoples Day of Action.

The NCMAC also set up at the first meeting our own New Cross Massacre Fact Finding Commission to check out all the facts concerning the massacre. We did not trust the police to carry out a proper investigation or to inform the press, radio and television correctly about what had taken place. This was our own action to provide alternative news and information to the press and tv. It broke the police monopoly of planting their own biased information in the media.

On the same Sunday, January 18th 1981, the New Cross Fire Fund was established by the main members of the NCMAC so as to raise some funds for the parents and families of the dead and injured, to assist them in their deep sorrow and to help them bury their dead. The entire amount of £27,000 collected was distributed among the families of the dead and injured.

The NCMAC also met after the funerals with the parents and formed them into the independent New Cross Fire Parents Committee so that they, after the burial of their children, could decide what they wanted and then act in their own interests.

Right from the beginning the metropolitan police denied there was any racist motive for the fire, even though a policeman had told Mrs Ruddock, at whose home the party was held, on the morning of the massacre that a firebomb had caused the fire. And in the week before the Black Peoples Day of Action they tried to undermine the Black Peoples Day of Action by claiming they had evidence that some black boys in a fight at the party had caused the fire. This was proven to be a police frameup and usual concoction of evidence during the coroners inquest. This police tactic did not work. Had the police admitted to what they had said in the first moments after the fire there would have been 100,000 people in the streets of London on Monday March 2nd 1981.

On Monday March 2nd 1981, 20,000 people marched for eight hours through the heart of London in the Black Peoples Day of Action – from Lewisham through Peckham, across Blackfriars Bridge, through Fleet Street, up Regent Street, down Cavendish Street to Marble Arch. A NCMAC delegation, led by the Committee's chairman, left the demonstration to deliver letters of protest about the Government's inaction to Members of Parliament at the House of Commons, to the Prime Minister at Downing Street, and to the Commissioner of the Metropolitan Police at Scotland Yard. **The New Cross Massacre Black People's Day of Action was and has been the largest and most effective demonstration of black political power in Britain to today's date. It was the watershed event in black history in Britain and it brought about major changes in British society.**

Immediately after the massacre and for many months after a family support group, including a black psychiatrist, psychotherapist, religious and social workers and others provided counselling and other emotional support for the members of the devastated families.

The NCMAC organised legal representation for the families during the 13 day long inquest held at County Hall. Their legal intervention foiled the plan of the police and coroner to prove that the massacre had not been the result of a racist attack. The coroners inquest jury returned an open verdict. Up to today, 10 years after, not a single person has been charged and brought to account for the New Cross Massacre. Over 50 police were assigned to the investigation of the cause of the fire and, on the word of the police, over £250,000 of taxpayers money was spent but with no result, or comfort for the parents and families and the black communities.

NEW CROSS MASSACRE ACTION COMMITTEE

BLACK PEOPLE'S DAY OF ACTION - MONDAY MARCH 2ND

STEWARDS' CODE OF BEHAVIOUR

1. Stewards should not drink alcohol or smoke ganja on the demonstration.
2. Stewards should wear distinctive armbands with the motif words 'stewards' and initials NCMAC. These should be approx. 6" x 4".
3. Armbands are to be produced from a central point.
4. Each organisation should provide 10 stewards.
5. Chief stewards should have special identification.
6. Stewards should approach members of the public in a polite manner and if there is dissent this should be reported to the chief steward.
7. The demonstration should walk about 8-10 abreast.
8. Stewards should have a detailed knowledge of route and should be furnished with information where first aid, toilets, lawyers and police stations are, and there should be a map that indicates these points clearly.
9. Stewards should not enter into any discussion with the police. That responsibility should be with the coordinators.
10. Stewards should stop any friendly or hostile dialogue with police.
11. Stewards should keep march moving even when the delegation departs for representation.
12. Stewards should always be between marchers and the police.
13. Stewards should not desert their posts or transfer their responsibility to somebody else, only with permission of steward in authority.
14. Stewards should know what banners are to be allowed in the demonstration.
15. Stewards are to be informed that white organisations are to march at the back of the demonstration.
16. Each organisation will nominate 5 observers to be known only to the coordinators and chief steward.
17. Stewards should know that the march is open to all ethnic groups.

PTO

Stewards' Code of Behaviour for the Black People's Day of Action March.

The route to be followed is as follows:

Fordham Park	St Georges Circus
Clifton Rise	Blackfriars Road
Edward Street	Blackfriars Bridge
Payne Street	New Bridge Street
Idonia Street	Ludgate Circus
Watson Street	Fleet Street
New Cross Road	Strand
Amersham Road	Aldwych (eastern arm)
Parkfield Road	Kingsway
Lewisham Way	High Holborn
New Cross Road	Shaftesbury Avenue
Queens Road	Piccadilly Circus (northside)
Peckham High Street	Regent Street
Clayton Road	Oxford Circus
Hanover Park	Regent Street
Rye Lane	Cavendish Place
Peckham High Street	Cavendish Square
Peckham Road	Wigmore Street
Camberwell Church Street	Portman Square
Camberwell Green (southside)	Seymour Street
Camberwell Green (westside)	Edgware Road
Camberwell Road	Tyburn Way
Walworth Road	Cumberland Gate
Elephant and Castle	Hyde Park (North Carriage Road)
St Georges Road	
Westminster Bridge Road	

The following parking arrangements have been made with the police:

Coaches dropping people for the demonstration can park in Marchant Street or Childeric Road

Coaches picking up demonstrators after the march can park in the North Carriage Road of Hyde Park.

PTO

Written agreement with the police over the route for the Black People's Day of Action March. An agreement which the police tried to unsuccessfully subvert when the March reached Blackfriars Bridge.

'THE NEW CROSS MASSACRE CAMPAIGN AND THE BLACK PEOPLE'S DAY OF ACTION DEMONSTRATION'

Black History Month talk given by Linton Kwesi Johnson and Michael La Rose at Goldsmiths University Student's Union, October 7th, 2010

Extract from The Black Peoples Day of Action March 1981 given by Michael La Rose

... I belonged to one of the main organisers of the march called The Alliance, which consisted of the Black Parents Movement, the Black Youth Movement and the Race Today Collective. However, the whole Black political spectrum was present in the New Cross Massacre campaign. Prominent were the Black Unity and Freedom Party – BUFP, PACM Head start along with left progressive organisations like Socialist Workers Party SWP. There were a wide range of political positions, but we worked hard at unity for action.

My father John La Rose was chair of the New Cross Massacre Action Committee and we ensured that the parents of the murdered young people were central to decisions made by the organisation. Through the Assembly, we worked out strategy, kept people informed of the latest facts along with the latest attempts by the police, and press to discredit the campaign and lie about the cause of the fire. We also organised up and down the country with groups and contacts developed over the years in campaigns to mobilise for the Black People's Day of Action demonstration. We all mobilised in colleges, student unions, youth clubs, community centres, sound systems, dance promoters, work places and unions. We issued leaflets like the one in the George Padmore Institute archives, which I hold up now, which we used to counter the lies and distortions of the press and police. We demanded that all organisations and individuals who supported the campaign bring banners and placards with words that reflected the main issues we were raising through the demonstration. We worked out chants and had a lorry and loud speakers on the march to make our message clearer and dynamic.

At the head of the march would be John La Rose and the parents of the murdered young people with large individual photos of the thirteen dead. This group would also act as the organisations delegation to Parliament and Downing Street.

We gathered at Fordham Park, on a grey Monday morning. There was constant rain, but without regard, people began to assemble. The heavy constant rain lasted through most of the day. The demonstration moved to 439 New Cross Road, then set off for Fleet Street, Regent Street and Hyde Park, via Peckham and Elephant and Castle. At every step, people joined the march, which was huge. It consisted of elderly people, young people, and babies in arms, young men, and the whole community. It consisted of all types of people but was about 90% black. When we reached a school in Peckham, the lively noisy march was joined by schoolchildren scaling the locked gates. This happened at most schools we passed.

We expected and planned for police disruption of the march and a test of our resolve. It duly came at Blackfriars Bridge. The Chartists also encountered resistance at Blackfriars Bridge to their march into London in the 1830s. On this day in 1981, the police formed a cordon behind riot shields across the road just before Blackfriars Bridge. They were stopping the demonstration. They were backed up by police vans as far as we could see going over the bridge. The demonstration had been agreed at the highest level yet the police now took this provocative action.

The chair and the parents had gone on a delegation to the Houses of Parliament, Scotland Yard and 10 Downing Street. The people at the front of the march began to throw missiles and scuffle with the police. The lorry with the loud speaker came right to the front of the march, calmed down the situation and demanded through chants and swaying that we be allowed to carry on our peaceful demonstration. The chants grew louder, the movement forward was stronger and persistent the march broke through the police cordon. The Metropolitan police decided to retreat. Their ranks opened up like the Red Sea. The police positioned on the bridge in the vans belonged to the City of London Police force. As the Met succumbed to the force and will of the march, the City of London police melted away. There was a huge cheer, and the front of the march ran unencumbered across Blackfriars Bridge. We called this event the 'Battle of Blackfriars'. We knew, as poet Linton Kwesi Johnson would say, 'We were making history'. The demonstration flooded into Fleet Street where the chants against the British press were fierce, loud and clear.

The march moved from the City into the West End, up Regent Street and into Great Cavendish Street. Here some people lost discipline and smashed a jewellery shop window. However, the marchers and the stewards quickly stopped this activity. The peaceful and disciplined demonstration ended in a rally in Hyde Park. The New Cross Massacre Black People's Day of

Action demonstration was a demonstration of great significance. It also gave the black population of Britain enormous confidence. ...

NEW CROSS MASSACRE
12 DEAD 27 INJURED

SUPPORT
Black Peoples
Day Of Action
DEMONSTRATE
On March 2nd 1981

Assemble at 10am at
Fordham Park next to Moonshot Community Centre Pagnell Street London SE14

Demonstration Moves From
439 New Cross Road to Fleet Street, Scotland Yard, House of Commons and 10 Downing Street ending in Hyde Park

STAND UP AGAINST THE MASS MURDER OF BLACK PEOPLE
STAND UP AGAINST ATTACKS BY WHITE RACISTS ON BLACK PEOPLE
STAND UP AGAINST THE BRITISH MOVEMENT, THE NATIONAL FRONT AND COLUMN 88
STAND UP AGAINST THE LIES AND CONFUSION SPREAD BY NEWSPAPERS, RADIO AND TELEVISION
STAND UP FOR THE RIGHTS OF BLACK PEOPLE TO HAVE THEIR PARTIES WITHOUT INTERFERENCE
WE WILL NOT LET THE POLICE PLAY AROUND WITH OUR LIVES

Issued by the New Cross Massacre Action Committee, c/o.74 Shakespeare Road, London SE24. Tel: 01-737 2268
British Rail and Underground Nearest Trains: New Cross and New Cross Gate Buses: 171, 53, 36, 36a, 36b, 141, 177, 21.

Flyer for a 30th Anniversary Event commemorating the New Cross Massacre Fire held at The Albany Theatre in Deptford on 14 January 2011.